Literature written for young adults...

by young adults.

Allow yourself to be surprised.

Breaking Barriers

Young Writers Chapbook Series

Louis Burts

Press

Atlanta

Cover design by Susan Arauz Barnes
Editing by Derek Koehl and Tavares Stephens
ISBN: 978-0-9856451-9-9

VerbalEyze Press books are available at special discounts for bulk purchases in the United States by corporations, institutions and other organizations.

For information, address VerbalEyze Press, 1376 Fairbanks Street SW, Atlanta, Georgia 30310.

VerbalEyze does not participate, endorse, or have any authority or responsibility concerning private correspondence between our authors and the public. All mail addressed to authors are forwarded, but the publisher cannot, unless specifically instructed by the author, give out an address or phone number.

VerbalEyze Press
A division of VerbalEyze, Inc.
www.verbaleyze.org

I would like to dedicate this book to my sisters Mariah and Samara and my mother Carresha.

Thank you for all the love and support you have given me over the years.

Table of Contents

Foreword 11

Editors' Note 13

Breaking Barriers 15

Experience.. 17

Warning.. 19

Imprisoned... 21

The Streets... 23

Original 25

Myth... 27

Freedom 29

Love.. 33

True Cure 35

It's Over.. 37

Certain of Me... 39

Breaking Barriers

Foreword

Many a black and white speckled notebook has been privy to the growing pains of young artists. They sketch, narrate, poet and rhyme to make sense of the world and orient themselves to the gravitational pull of coming of age. But their musings beg for answers and an empathetic head nod, so Ya-Heard? Poetics was born.

Whether speaking heartache at the mic, spitting social commentary over tracks or texting observations into the ether, the power and influence of word is undeniable and YaHeard? Poets study the craft, explore their creative process and learn how to promote their artistic endeavors through collaborations with organizations like VerbalEyze, a beacon for young artists.

YaHeard? was founded by Educator-Artists to support the creative stirrings of tweens and teens and the publication of this chapbook honors and encourages the work of a young artists whose passion and talent confirms them as part of a new generation of prolific writers, artists and musicians. Their musings have escaped from first notebooks and into your hands. Answer if you dare; head nod if you must ---this young scribe dares to explore the power of voice.

Ya Heard?

Susan Arauz Barnes
Co-founder, YaHeard? Poetics

Editors' Note

The Young Writers Chapbook Series is an expression of the mission and vision that is core to what we do at VerbalEyze. Through this series, we are able to provide talented, emerging young authors their debut introduction to the reading public. We are grateful that you also share an enthusiasm for young authors and the vibrant and energized perspectives they bring to our shared understanding of the human experience and what it means to live, love, long, lose and wonder as we travel together through this world.

We are pleased to bring to you an exceptional young writer, Regan Nesbit, with this edition of the Young Writers Chapbook. We trust that you will be as engaged and challenged by her words as we have been. Regan is part of an exceptional group of young writers, YaHeard? Poetics. She and her fellow writers are an never-ending encouragement and inspiration to us.

Read, enjoy and, as always, *allow yourself to be surprised.*

Derek Koehl
Tavares Stephens

Breaking Barriers

I'm just a little boy hidden from your eyes

Surrounded by lies

When my spirit dies

My heart flies

In my mind

I'm dead

All these restrictions keep me in my head

Keep me in my bed

Where I can dream as I please

But when I wake up I leave

Dreams where I am a king

Return to being unseen

Experience

I've been around the block a lot

But never got mad or fought

I kept it cool

Even though I was surrounded by fools

Fighting doesn't solve anything

And neither do insults

From experience passed down from my elders

I can become an example

Warning

Money is the reason

For evil and treason

And terroristic acts

'Cause they just want fat stacks

And they won't relax until they have all that

Life is all about trial and error

Not fancy cars and mirrors

Which are imported

But to afford it

The buyer resorted

To violence

So to silence

His victims

He loaded a gun

Walked in

And pulled the trigger

Once

As a warning

Then took the money

And like a coward ran and hid for hours

Fell into despair like the Twin Towers

For a couple hundred bucks

Imprisoned

Crack will become your name

If you play that game

You'll be a thug

Use drugs for love

You'll be doing time

And out of line

A slave to addictive desires

Living in a prison

Off of three meals a day

But this isn't Jonah and the Whale

You could've even gone to Yale

And still be eligible for jail

The Streets

Stay on your toes

Who knows

What may happen in the streets

It's an incredible feat

To escape the streets

Where there is poverty

Everywhere

And a government that doesn't care

About the welfare

Of the streets

Original

Life is skeptical, a miracle, something worth cheering for

It does suck sometimes, but not when I'm busting rhymes

Sure there is pain, but life is a game worth playing

I'm just saying

No need in complaining

When everybody hates on you

Don't act like you're a bug and they're a shoe

'Cause you'll get through

All the grief and pain that can hit like a train

And holds you in chains

You can break

Because you're really something

You are

Original

Myth

wings like wisdom

sun like tempting

outright disobedience

the downfall.

follow the usual path

not so close to the sun

don't listen

fall

Freedom

Is freedom of speech what we teach?

Or something we want

People are always telling children what to say

Our voices are ignored across the world

In every single way

Forced to be child slaves

And go to their graves

Their lives reduced to just pawns

And to sit by

Isn't right

Why do we believe in freedoms?

If many don't even have them

Like child soldiers

With the weight of AK-47's on their shoulders

The grief must be so choking

Forced to fight without reason

Except treason

Their lives are miserable

While we sit here and make them invisible

A person must be truly evil

To do this to our young people

They don't get education

And live in war torn nations

And to sit by

Isn't right

Why do we believe in freedoms?

If many don't even have them

Like Syria, where children are being slaughtered

Because of their fathers'

Desire for freedom

Now we must give it to them

Louis Burts

Love

Love can't be changed

Not fake, stupid, or lame

Kindness has no shame

Understand this

Drill it in your brain

Love is the opposite of shame

This is the road to fame

And depending on how you play the game

Love will bring honor to your name

True Cure

Got me on all these medications

What I need is meditation

On the one true God

Who shed blood

Even though He could have forgotten us

And left us messed up

He did not have to save us

Die, bleed for us

Or even breathe for us

So the only medicine I need

Is Christ rooting for me

Don't you see?

It's not about sinners

Like me

With P.H.D's

Don't you see

It's about the one who set us free

Jesus has healed me!

It's Over

It's over

My life

Is there anything I regret?

Well, I do regret not graduating yet

Or listening to my mother

And being rude to my family and friends

I regret not taking chances

And trying new things

If I could just do it again…

Then I wake up

"Wow! I better live my life to the fullest.

Because, sooner or later, it's over."

Certain of Me

I used to be a zero

Now I'm a hero

Discussing the creativity in me

Now I'm flying higher

Than a fire can burn through your soul

Leaving behind an empty hole

And to fill my soul I go looking

For something

Though I know who makes the beginning and end

It's up to me to make the in-between inspirational

And leave my impression of everything sensational

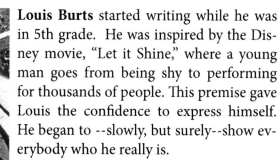

Louis Burts started writing while he was in 5th grade. He was inspired by the Disney movie, "Let it Shine," where a young man goes from being shy to performing for thousands of people. This premise gave Louis the confidence to express himself. He began to --slowly, but surely--show everybody who he really is.

He enjoys spending time with his family, reading, and writing for fun. He loves the *Diary of a Wimpy Kid* series and enjoys watching the avant-garde shows on Cartoon Network like the *Regular Show* and *Amazing World of Gumball*.

Louis happily resides with his mother and two sisters in Atlanta, Georgia where he writes, learns, and inspires.

Photo credit: arauzingink

Empowering young writers to say, **"I am my scholarship!"**

Open call for submissions to the *Young Writers Anthology*!

See your work in print!

Become a published writer!

**Earn royalites that can help
you pay for college!s**

VerbalEyze Press is accepting submissions from young adult writers, ages 13 to 22, in any of the following genres:

- poetry
- short story
- songwriting
- playwriting
- graphic novel
- creative non-fiction

For submission details, visit
www.verbaleyze.org

VerbalEyze serves to foster, promote and support the development and professional growth of emerging young writers.

Writers Cooperative

VerbalEyze is a nonprofit organization whose mission is to foster, promote and support the development and professional growth of emerging young writers.

The *Young Writers Anthology* is published as a service of VerbalEyze in furtherance of its goal to provide young writers with access to publishing opportunities that they otherwise would not have.

Fifty percent of the proceeds received from the sale of the *Young Writers Anthology* are paid to the authors in the form of scholarships to help them advance in their post-secondary education.

For more information about VerbalEyze and how you can become involved in its work with young writers, visit www.verbaleyze.org.